ONENESS

ONENESS

GREAT PRINCIPLES SHARED BY ALL RELIGIONS

JEFFREY MOSES

FAWCETT COLUMBINE • NEW YORK

Grateful acknowledgment
is made to the National Council
of the Churches of Christ in the USA
for permission to reprint from the Revised
Standard Version Bible. Copyright 1946, 1952,
© 1971 by the Division of Christian
Education of the National Council
of the Churches of Christ in the
USA. Used by permission.

Library of Congress Catalog
Card Number: 92-90071

ISBN: 0-449-90760-0

Design by Holly Johnson
Manufactured in the United States of America

First Trade Paperback Edition:
10 9 8 7 6 5 4 3 2

To Ruth, whose love and devotion
helped bring this book to light.

Every major religion of the world has similar ideals of love, the same goal of benefitting humanity through spiritual practice, and the same effect of making their followers into better human beings. As this book shows, the great religious teachers wanted to lead people away from the paths of misdeeds caused by ignorance and introduce them to paths of goodness.

THE DALAI LAMA

CONTENTS

ONENESS

FOREWORD

Throughout the ages, the scriptures of all religions have proclaimed that humanity is one great family. This is a simple truth, and it is simply and directly stated in every religion. In fact, almost all the principles that are associated with religious thought are shared by every religion. The Golden Rule, Love Thy Neighbor, Honor Thy Father and Mother, Speak Truth, It Is More Blessed to Give Than to Receive—these principles and others are common to all religions and are very similarly expressed in each.

This book discusses many of these fundamental precepts and shows their similarity of expression. Each page was put together with the awareness that modern words can hardly add to the immensity of the world's collected spiritual wisdom. For this reason the commentaries are short, allowing the sayings to speak for themselves.

The principles in this book form the basis for structuring an individual's life. The great sayings are like a guide or a blueprint for the inner development of mind and spirit that allows a person to achieve his highest goals. These principles are the foundation for success in personal relationships with family and friends, for satisfaction and success in business activities, and for that final aspiration in life that each person ultimately desires—the achievement of inner peace extending beyond the confines of an individual lifetime.

These great principles are not limiting to a person's satisfaction and fulfillment. Instead, they are guidelines that enable men and women to evolve to the highest point of human consciousness, wherein oneness is achieved with all the laws of nature. They allow men to avoid mistakes, to take the path of growth and achievement, and to answer the urgent and vital questions that ultimately arise.

Many people today seek their own laws. Yet in so doing, they often find only partial values of these universal principles. In actu-

ality, the full values of these universal principles have been recorded similarly in all
major religions since time immemorial. The
principles of inner development are basi-
cally no different now than they were in the
days of Jesus, Buddha, Muhammad, Shankara, or Confucious. These great masters
offer similar messages that have not become
less essential for people in the modern
world. These principles stretch beyond time
and change. They establish a clearly marked
path which will enable each individual to
attain the peace and enlightenment that is
the ultimate goal in life.

THE GOLDEN RULE

The Golden Rule is the cornerstone of religious understanding. Such diverse principles as *Love Thy Neighbor, Honor Thy Father and Mother, Speak Truth, Judge Not, Do Not Harm Anyone,* and *It Is More Blessed to Give Than To Receive*—among many others—are reflections of The Golden Rule. Abiding by The Golden Rule in thought and in deed naturally evokes the expression of all these other principles.

The Golden Rule is the most succinct and all-embracing description of how individuals and nations should act toward their neighbors. Every religion considers The Golden Rule to be the highest expression of spiritual thought. The founders of every major world religion—among them Jesus, Buddha, Krishna, Confucius, and Muhammad—all taught that following The Golden Rule is the surest way for mankind to fulfill its most cherished ideals.

THE GOLDEN RULE

Do unto others as you would have them
do unto you, for this is the law and the
prophets.

Christianity

What is hurtful to yourself do not to your
fellow man. That is the whole of the
Torah and the remainder is but
commentary.

Judaism

Do unto all men as you would wish to
have done unto you; and reject for others
what you would reject for yourselves.

Islam

Hurt not others with that which pains
yourself.

Buddhism

Tzu-Kung asked: "Is there one principle
upon which one's whole life may proceed?"
The Master replied, "Is not Reciprocity
such a principle?—what you do not
yourself desire, do not put before others."

Confucianism

This is the sum of all true righteousness—
Treat others, as thou wouldst thyself be
    treated.
Do nothing to thy neighbor, which
    hereafter
Thou wouldst not have thy neighbor do
    to thee.

Hinduism

HONOR THY FATHER
AND MOTHER

It would be difficult to repay our parents for the hours, days, and years they cared for us when we were young. Perhaps the only way to return some of that love is through caring for our own children, and for our parents as they grow older.

We should do our best to know our parents, for knowing them is the key to knowing ourselves. The day will come when we shall wish we had known them better.

HONOR THY FATHER
AND MOTHER

My son, keep your father's commandment,
and forsake not your mother's teaching.
Bind them upon your heart always; tie
them about your neck. When you walk,
they will lead you; when you lie down,
they will watch over you; and when you
awake, they will talk with you.

Judaism

For God commanded, saying, Honor thy
father and mother.

Christianity

Honor thy Father and Mother. Forget not
the favours thou hast received.

Hinduism

Serve and revere your parents. Heaven is
spread beneath the feet of mothers
everywhere.

Islam

To support Father and Mother,
To cherish Wife and Child,
To follow a peaceful calling,
This is the greatest blessing.

Buddhism

If each man would love his parents and
show due respect to his elders, the whole
empire would enjoy tranquillity.

Confucianism

THERE IS ONE GOD

Nature, Being, the Absolute, or an actual name for God—whatever term man uses, his almost universal belief that there is one God shows a profound oneness of the human spirit.

Such a belief reveals a conviction that an ultimate existence pervades all the boundaries of the universe, and that all people and all things are of one essence.

THERE IS ONE GOD

There is one God and Father of all, who is above all, and through all, and in you all.

Christianity

Have we not all one Father? Has not one God created us?

Judaism

He is the one God hidden in all beings, all-pervading, the Self within all beings, watching over all worlds, dwelling in all beings, the witness, the perceiver.

Hinduism

Remember even when alone that the Divine is everywhere.

Confucianism

There is but one God whose name is true. He is the creator, immortal, unborn, self-existent.

Sikhism

SPEAK TRUTH

A man cannot be untruthful in one area of his life without having that influence permeate every other sphere. Untruthfulness creates habits in the personality that ultimately affect everything that a man wishes to accomplish. A man cannot speak lies while at work and then, later in the day, be entirely truthful with his family. Love and inner growth are enhanced by speaking truthfully. If only for personal fulfillment, a man should cultivate truthfulness in all aspects of his life.

On another level no less important, untruthfulness indicates an ignorance of the intrinsic oneness of all people. An individual will lie only when he thinks that he is separate from others and that he can make a significant advancement in life by impeding the progress of others. Any advantage gained by untruthfulness is temporary at best, because the most fundamental and important activity in life—the development of an awareness of God—is impeded by deceit.

SPEAK TRUTH

Putting away lying, speak every man truth with his neighbor: for we are members one of another.

Christianity

Speak ye every man truth to his neighbor; execute the judgment of truth and peace in your gates.

Judaism

Him I call indeed a Brahmana who utters true speech, instructive and free from harshness, so that he offends no one.

Buddhism

Do not clothe the truth with falsehood;
do not knowingly conceal the truth.

Islam

Say what is true! Do thy duty. Do not
swerve from the truth.

Hinduism

Sincerity is the way of Heaven, and to
think how to be sincere is the way of a
man. Never was there one possessed of
complete sincerity who did not move
others. Never was there one without
sincerity who was able to move others.

Confucianism

MORE BLESSED TO
GIVE THAN TO RECEIVE

The wise handling of money can be as spiritually enriching as prayer. A person who is in touch with his own inner self and who truly loves his fellow man will experience his heart spontaneously overflowing with the desire to care for others.

The giving of money, time, support, and encouragement to worthy causes can never be detrimental to the giver. The laws of nature are structured so that acts of charity will open an individual to an unbounded reservoir of riches. Everything in life has been created as the result of love and concern for others. When individuals give lovingly to their brothers in the family of man, they establish the basis for peace within every nation.

MORE BLESSED TO GIVE THAN TO RECEIVE

It is more blessed to give than to receive.

Christianity

Extend your help without seeking reward.
Give to others and do not regret or
begrudge your liberality. Those who are
thus are good.

Taoism

In the minds of the generous
contentment is produced.

Sikhism

The poor, the orphan, the captive—feed them for the love of God alone, desiring no reward, nor even thanks.

Islam

Bounteous is he who gives to the beggar who comes to him in want of food and feeble.

Hinduism

Blessed is he that considereth the poor: the Lord will deliver him in time of trouble.

Judaism

HEAVEN IS
WITHIN

Life is structured so that the finest, most meaningful aspects are often hidden from outer exposure. The sweetness of an orange is hidden within a bitter skin. The seed of a tree, from which life will spring, is protected within a hard shell. And a man may walk the earth, not knowing that a vast depository of riches lies hidden deep within the ground beneath his feet.

From earliest childhood our senses respond to outward sensations. Without guidance and understanding, we could spend a lifetime appreciating the world only in an outward direction. But the true riches of life lie within. Through appreciation of the wisdom of the past, through prayer, and, most of all, through deep meditation, we can become one with the inner silence that is a part of God.

When that silence is reached, it begins to

radiate throughout all of one's activities. When a large number of individuals radiate this inner silence, heaven will begin to be seen on earth.

HEAVEN IS WITHIN

The kingdom of God cometh not with observation: neither shall they say, Lo here! or, lo there! for, behold, the kingdom of God is within you.

Christianity

What the undeveloped man seeks is outside; what the advanced man seeks is within himself.

Confucianism

If you think the Law is outside yourself, you are embracing not the absolute Law but some inferior teaching.

Buddhism

Do not search in distant skies for God.
In man's own heart is He found.

Shintoism

God bides hidden in the hearts of all.

Hinduism

Why wilt thou go into the jungles? What
do you hope to find there? Even as the
scent dwells within the flower, so God
within thine own heart ever abides. Seek
Him with earnestness and find Him there.

Sikhism

LOVE THY
NEIGHBOR

Every human being is born with an innate love for others. As a person matures, this love is put to many tests. Yet by understanding the teachings of the world's great religions, a person can find the faith he needs for his love to endure beyond life's hardships.

More than a passing glance at the scriptures is necessary to achieve this level of understanding. Acts of faith, prayer, and deep meditation provide us with the strength that allows love for our fellow man to become an abiding part of our lives, of our beings. When many of us attain this type of faith, the expression of love in the world will be as spontaneous and natural as love between mother and child.

LOVE THY NEIGHBOR

Thou shalt love thy neighbor as thyself.
Judaism

A new commandment I give to you, That you love one another; even as I have loved you . . . By this all men will know that you are my disciples, if you have love for one another.
Christianity

A man obtains a proper rule of action by looking on his neighbor as himself.
Hinduism

Full of love for all things in the world,
practicing virtue in order to benefit
others, this man alone is happy.

Buddhism

Seek to be in harmony with all your
neighbors; live in amity with your
brethren.

Confucianism

Regard Heaven as your father, Earth as
your mother, and all things as your
brothers and sisters.

Shintoism

CONQUER
WITH LOVE

Whenever there is tension or fighting between individuals, groups, or nations, it means that a time of mutual understanding has been lost, and channels of communication have not been used.

Love is a unifying force. It radiates outward to resolve differences between people and nations. It is not that these unique qualities dissolve and are lost, but that they are integrated into a greater whole in which they are made more useful and beautiful.

Love conquers *before* there is fighting. Even if channels of communication have broken down and fighting breaks out, the underlying attitude should still be one of love and unification by love.

CONQUER
WITH LOVE

Recompense evil, conquer it, with good.

Islam

Be not overcome of evil, but overcome
evil with good.

Christianity

With kindness conquer rage, with
goodness malice; with generosity defeat
all meanness; with the straight truth
defeat lies and deceit.

Hinduism

A soft answer turns away wrath, but a harsh word stirs up anger.

Judaism

Conquer your foe by force, and you increase his anger. Conquer by love, and you will reap no after-sorrow.

Buddhism

Love is sure to be victorious even in battle, and firmly to maintain its ground. Heaven will save its possessor, by his love protecting him.

Taoism

BLESSED ARE THE PEACEMAKERS

When people live in the awareness that there is a close kinship between all individuals and nations, peace is the natural result. Peace can come about only as a result of concern and understanding for others. It can never be brought about by superficial negotiation or temporary agreement.

Peace certainly cannot be brought about by signatures on pieces of paper. Since the beginning of recorded history, tens of thousands of peace treaties have been signed between nations. Clearly, treaties cannot sustain peace. This is a lesson that must be learned finally and absolutely. It is time now to look toward deeper, more lasting feelings of love and understanding between people. This and this alone can bring sustained harmony in the world.

BLESSED ARE THE
PEACEMAKERS

Blessed are the peacemakers: for they
shall be called the children of God.

Christianity

Shall I tell you what acts are better than
fasting, charity, and prayers? Making
peace between enemies are such acts; for
enmity and malice tear up the heavenly
rewards by the roots.

Islam

The noble minded dedicate themselves to
the promotion of peace and the
happiness of others—even those who
injure them.

Hinduism

When righteousness is practiced to win
peace, he who so walks shall gain the
victory and all fetters utterly destroy.

Buddhism

How beautiful upon the mountains are
the feet of him who brings good tidings,
who publishes peace.

Judaism

AS YE SOW, SO SHALL YE REAP

This is the great mystery of human life. This principle is so fundamental to each person's desires and goals that it forms a framework for activity throughout the day. For those who are aware that this principle is the determining factor in achieving happiness and success, the hours of the day become an attempt to act toward others with kindness and rightness. Those who are unaware struggle continuously throughout their lives and do not know why. Aware or unaware, all are ruled by this inevitable law of nature.

AS YE SOW, SO SHALL YE REAP

It is nature's rule, that as we sow, we shall reap.

Buddhism

Whatever a man sows, that he will also reap.

Christianity

A liberal man will be enriched, and one who waters will himself be watered.

Judaism

What proceeds from you will return to
you.

Confucianism

Thou canst not gather what thou dost
not sow; as thou dost plant the tree so it
will grow.

Hinduism

Whatever man soweth, that shall he reap.
If he soweth trouble, trouble shall be his
harvest. If a man sow poison, he cannot
expect ambrosia.

Sikhism

A MAN IS KNOWN BY HIS DEEDS, NOT BY HIS RELIGION

Inner life is the basis for outer activity. A person's actions are the mirror of his inner self. For this reason, when a man achieves an understanding of the spiritual aspects of human life, he spontaneously acts in a manner that encourages and supports a similar development of this knowledge in others. We need look no deeper than a man's outer activity to see the degree of his inner spiritual achievement.

A MAN IS KNOWN BY HIS DEEDS, NOT BY HIS RELIGION

God will not ask a man of what race he is. He will ask what he has done.

Sikhism

God will render to every man according to his deeds.

Christianity

A man asked Muhammad how to tell when one is truly faithful, and he replied: "If you derive pleasure from the good which you do and are grieved by the evil which you commit, then you are a true believer."

Islam

But I say unto you: deeds of love are
worth as much as all the commandments
of the law.

Judaism

No brahmin is a brahmin by birth.
No outcaste is an outcaste by birth.
An outcaste is an outcaste by his deeds.
A brahmin is a brahmin by his deeds.

Buddhism

NOT WORDS OR DETACHMENT, BUT ACTION

It is necessary, and perhaps one of our primary tasks on earth, to actively resolve the differences and disagreements between people.

Each person should have the goal to depart from this life having removed from the world all need for locks and keys and weapons and armor.

This goal may be too idealistic for many people—yet if no one on earth holds such an ideal, a state of peace and harmony will never reign on earth.

NOT WORDS OR DETACHMENT, BUT ACTION

Not everyone that sayeth, Lord, Lord, shall enter into the kingdom of heaven; but he that doeth the will of my Father which is in heaven.

Christianity

Not learning but doing is the chief thing.

Judaism

Not in words does God get answers.

Taoism

Students and teachers, and all others,
Who read the mere words of ponderous
    books, know nothing,
But only waste their time in vain pursuit
    of words;
He who acts righteously is wise.

                                 Hinduism

Like a beautiful flower, full of color, but
without scent, are the fine but fruitless
words of him who does not act
accordingly.

                                Buddhism

BETTER TO
EXAMINE THE SELF

 Our activities and successes are based on our inner strength and wholeness. To grow, it is necessary for us to recognize and correct our own faults. Yet it is difficult to do this since we hide our shortcomings not only from others but from ourselves.

When we gain the ability to recognize and correct our own bad habits, we begin to make rapid strides toward greater happiness and success in all spheres of life. Only by learning to admit to our own faults can we become more tolerant and loving to our fellow man and to his shortcomings.

BETTER TO
EXAMINE THE SELF

If you love others, and affection is not
returned, look into your love. If you rule
others, and they are unruly, look into
your wisdom. If you treat others politely
and they do not return your politeness,
look into your respect. If your desires are
not fulfilled, turn inward and examine
yourself.

Confucianism

First take the log out of your own eye,
and then you will see clearly to take the
speck out of your brother's eye.

Christianity

The faults of others we see easily; our own are very difficult to see. Our neighbour's faults we winnow eagerly, as chaff from grain; our own we hide away as a cheat hides a losing roll of the dice.

Buddhism

He who knows others is discerning; he who knows himself is wise.

Taoism

They who quarrel with others, instead of quarreling with their own hearts, waste their lives.

Sikhism

BETTER TO RULE
THE SPIRIT

Through the ages, saints and sages of all religions have proclaimed that the human soul is unbounded and eternal. However different in outer expression, all religions have their source in this fundamental belief. Deep within each person is an individual consciousness that touches and is a part of the Universal Consciousness. Religion is that which allows this connection to be brought into our immediate awareness, and to be used practically in our day-to-day lives.

Since the length of an individual lifetime is brief compared to the infinity of time, it is wise to dedicate ourselves to the highest of goals.

BETTER TO RULE
THE SPIRIT

For what is a man profited, if he shall gain the whole world, and lose his own soul?

Christianity

He who is slow to anger is better than the mighty, and he who rules his spirit than he who takes a city.

Judaism

If one were to conquer in battle a thousand times a thousand men, he who conquers himself is the greatest warrior.

Buddhism

He who restrains his rage from bolting
   with him,
He is true warrior and true charioteer,
Not he who slays in battle many foes.

Hinduism

He who overcomes others is strong; he
who overcomes himself is mighty.

Taoism

Difficult to conquer is one's self. But
when that is conquered, everything is
conquered.

Jainism

WISDOM IS MORE
THAN RICHES

Wisdom is not a vague quality of mind. It is not a mood of resignation or detachment. Wisdom is a combination of experience and awareness that gives great dynamism to every activity undertaken. It is inner strength, intuitive creativity, and mental power. Wisdom allows a person to evaluate experiences of the past in a clear and orderly manner so that he can avoid further mistakes. It allows a person to look so deeply into present activities that glimpses of the future can be seen.

In the fullest sense, wisdom is a state of consciousness. Wisdom dawns when a person experiences the connection of his or her individual awareness with the Infinite. Then life is lived in the light of God, and all his undertakings are completely successful and fulfilling.

WISDOM IS MORE
THAN RICHES

Riches are not from an abundance of
worldly goods, but from a contented
mind.

Islam

Lay not up for yourselves treasures upon
earth, where moth and rust doth corrupt,
and where thieves break through and
steal. But lay up for yourselves treasures
in heaven, where neither moth nor rust
doth corrupt, and where thieves do not
break through nor steal: for where your
treasure is, there will your heart be also.

Christianity

The real treasure is that laid up by a man
or woman through charity and piety,
temperance and self control . . . The

treasure thus hid is secure, and does not pass away.

Buddhism

How much better is it to get wisdom than gold! and to get understanding rather than silver!

Judaism

Knowledge is the best treasure that a man can secretly hoard in life. Learning is the revered of the revered. It is learning alone that enables a man to better the conditions of his friends and relations. Knowledge is the holiest of the holies, the god of the gods, and commands respect of crowned heads; shorn of it man is but an animal.

Hinduism

MAN DOES NOT LIVE
BY BREAD ALONE

The blessings of life are deeper than what can be appreciated by the senses. They are deeper even than what can be understood by the mind. Every aspect of life swirls with rhythms of the Divine. All activities, all successes, all well-being and happiness, have their basis in an unfathomable Spirit which sustains us even when we are not aware of it.

The fullest expression of the Divine is found in loving relationships between people. Life is nourished by kindness, by concern for others, by forgiving, by sharing, and by caring for all of God's creatures. Man does not live by material bread alone. He lives by a deeper power, one that creates and supports all the functions of life.

Man can express the fullness of the Divine. Every act of good, no matter how small, helps radiate the Divine throughout the world. The closer a person can come towards harmony with this power—with this spirit of the Divine—the more joy life will have for him.

MAN DOES NOT LIVE
BY BREAD ALONE

Man shall not live by bread alone, but by
every word of God.

Christianity

Man lives not by material bread alone.

Hinduism

Make divine knowledge thy food.

Sikhism

Man doth not live by bread only, but by every word that proceedeth out of the mouth of the Lord.

Judaism

The superior man deliberates upon how he may walk in truth, not upon what he may eat.

Confucianism

DO NOT HARM ANYTHING

Just as we try to nourish and strengthen ourselves, so we should do the same for others. If someone tries to hurt another, it means that he is perceiving that person as something separate and foreign from himself.

We must remember that the feelings and hopes of others are the same as ours. Do not forget that all religions—which convey mankind's highest thoughts and aspirations—view all the people in the world as one great family.

DO NOT HARM ANYTHING

Do not hurt others, do no one injury by thought or deed, utter no word to pain thy fellow creatures.

Hinduism

Hurt none by word or deed, be consistent in well-doing.

Buddhism

Be ye kind to one another, tenderhearted, forgiving one another, even as God for Christ's sake hath forgiven you.

Christianity

Master of his senses and avoiding wrong,
one should do no harm to any living
being, neither by thoughts nor words nor
acts.

Jainism

Whatever good you do for others, you
send it before your own soul and shall
find it with God, who sees all you do.

Islam

BLESSED TO
FORGIVE

How often does a mother forgive her infant? How often did Jesus forgive wrong? How often did Buddha, Muhammad, Shankara, and other enlightened teachers smile forgivingly at the faults of others?

We all will err at some point as we work through the lessons we must learn. Forgiveness is as necessary to life as the food we eat and the air we breathe. When an individual can cultivate an attitude of forgiveness, he helps to create a pocket of tranquillity in the world.

An attitude of forgiveness fosters channels of love and understanding in the heart. Years of education involving the study of books, laws and sayings cannot culture the intellect and emotions as can an attitude of forgiveness. Practicing forgiveness of others creates a habit that ultimately allows us to forgive events in our own past. Only then can life blossom into the fullness we desire.

BLESSED TO
FORGIVE

The most beautiful thing a man can do is
to forgive wrong.

Judaism

Then Peter came up and said to him,
"Lord, how often shall my brother sin
against me, and I forgive him? As many
as seven times?" Jesus said to him, "I do
not say to you seven times, but seventy
times seven."

Christianity

Forgive thy servant seventy times a day.

Islam

Where there is forgiveness there is God himself.

Sikhism

Recompense injury with kindness.

Taoism

Never is hate diminished by hatred;
It is only diminished by love—
This is an eternal law.

Buddhism

BE SLOW
TO ANGER

Anger clouds the mind in the very moments that clarity and objectivity are needed most. Anger is the enemy of success and satisfaction. It rips apart the contented feeling in the mind. The more a person can stand apart and control sudden anger, the greater the chance for success in any undertaking, and the greater the chance for lasting fulfillment in life.

In the deepest sense, anger shows that a person feels he or she alone—not God—is responsible for the end result of an activity. Such a person can become very frustrated when obstacles suddenly arise. By remembering that there are many elements involved in success over which a person has little control, he can learn to diminish the fire of anger.

It has been said that when angry with loved ones, a person should count to ten before speaking. Actually, counting to ten is not long enough. Don't speak until calmness has been regained. If this takes an hour, or several hours, it is better than saying something that may be deeply regretted.

BE SLOW
TO ANGER

He who is slow to anger has great understanding, but he who has a hasty temper exalts folly.

Judaism

He who gives up anger attains to God.

Hinduism

Let not the sun go down upon your wrath.

Christianity

Let us cease from wrath and refrain from angry gestures.

Shintoism

He who holds back rising anger like a rolling chariot, him I call a real driver; others only hold the reins.

Buddhism

JUDGE NOT

Great philosophers have analyzed this principle for thousands of years, but for the person who is kind and thoughtful toward others, the meaning is simple and clear.

Like "As ye sow, so shall ye reap," and The Golden Rule, this principle is an expression of the underlying truth that mankind is one great family, and that we all spring from a common source.

JUDGE NOT

Judge not, and ye shall not be judged:
condemn not, and ye shall not be
condemned: forgive, and ye shall be
forgiven.

Christianity

Judge not thy neighbor till thou art in his
place.

Judaism

Judge not thy neighbor.

Buddhism

Follow that which is revealed to thee, and persevere with patience until God shall judge; for he is the best judge.

Islam

FOLLOW THE SPIRIT OF THE SCRIPTURES, NOT THE LETTER

Individual religions, like different nations and cultures, have unique characteristics. But these characteristics are only the surface aspects; the fundamental principles at the heart of all religions (like those at the core of all cultures and nations) are universal.

For this reason, the letters of the law, or the surface meanings found in the words of the teachings, are not as integral as the spirit of the law, which is universal and shared by all religions and cultures.

FOLLOW THE SPIRIT
OF THE SCRIPTURES,
NOT THE LETTER

The letter killeth, but the spirit giveth life.
Christianity

Rather let a letter be uprooted than the
Torah be forgotten.

Judaism

The Koran was sent down in seven
dialects, and in every one of its sentences
there is an outer and an inner meaning.

Islam

Study the words, no doubt, but look
Behind them to the thought they indicate,
And having found it, throw the words
   away
As chaff when you have sifted out the
   grain.

Hinduism

Let not scholars scrutinize
The language of the wise too closely;
The seers think more of the thought
Than of the words in which 'tis caught.

Sufism

START WHEN YOUNG
TO SEEK WISDOM

When a seed germinates, it first sends a root downward into the earth. Only when the root is firmly established do limbs and branches begin to form. When constructing a skyscraper that will tower hundreds of feet in the air, builders first dig into the ground. Only when the foundation is complete does upward construction begin.

The same is true in a young person's growth. The stronger and more orderly the inner preparation, the greater the chance for fulfillment in life.

A great step is taken toward success and happiness when one becomes able to learn from the advice of others, not only from one's own successes and failures. Until that time, progress will be slow, and unnecessary suffering will result.

The most important advice to be understood and followed is the collected wisdom of the world's religions. This wisdom allows a person to establish an inner foundation for success and happiness. The younger a person is when he becomes aware of this, the easier it will be to accomplish all he wants in life.

START WHEN YOUNG
TO SEEK WISDOM

My son, gather instruction from thy
youth up; so shalt thou find wisdom till
thine old age.

Judaism

Knowledge is riches, what one learns in
youth is engraven on stone.

Hinduism

Seek ye first the kingdom of God, and
His righteousness; and all these things
shall be added unto you.

Christianity

Seek knowledge from the cradle to the grave.

Islam

He who, even as a young student, applies himself to the doctrine of truth, brightens up this world like the moon set free from the clouds.

Buddhism

BE WHOLEHEARTED

All success in life is the result of putting our attention into the proper channels and allowing a natural growth to occur. It is far too easy to let the mind remain divided, thinking about one thing or another, while trying to accomplish something important.

Working with a divided mind almost always gives results that are less than hoped for. But when a direct course is taken and a task is undertaken with dynamic, one-pointed perseverance, we can overcome even the most difficult obstacles.

BE WHOLEHEARTED

Wheresoever you go, employ all your
heart.

Confucianism

He who doubts is like a wave of the sea
that is driven and tossed by the wind.

Christianity

Whatever your hand finds to do, do it
with your might.

Judaism

Free yourself from doubt and you will find your life quickened in the goodness of God.

Shintoism

Neither eating, nor fasting, nor penance, nor sacrifice, nor observance of the seasons, purify a mortal who has not conquered his doubt.

Buddhism

HONOR THE
ELDERLY

It is not in nature's plan for the elderly to be overly active in society, but they contribute in very important ways to the achievements of a nation. The gathered knowledge of the elderly in practical matters is immense. No person who has specific goals and aspirations should disregard the advice of these experienced individuals.

The more the aspirations of a society are based on the true nature of happiness—the lasting inner oneness with all things—the more a society will honor its aged members. Wisdom fills the elderly like water fills a reservoir. For this wellspring to flow, we must maintain a pipeline of respect.

HONOR THE
ELDERLY

He who always greets and constantly
reveres the aged, four things will increase
to him: life, beauty, happiness, power.

Buddhism

With the ancient is wisdom; and in length
of days understanding.

Judaism

Treat with reverence due to age the elders
in your own family.

Confucianism

Rebuke not an elder, but intreat him as a father.

Christianity

To honor an old man is to show respect for God.

Islam

OUR TRUE
STRENGTH

Time exposes life's superficial aspects; only fundamental truths endure. When looking at ancient buildings, and monuments constructed thousands of years ago, we see that decorations and ornaments have vanished. Even walls and roofs have crumbled. Only foundations and central pillars remain. Similarly, the limbs and extremities of ancient statues often have fallen away, leaving only those portions supported by strong central structures.

The same is true in an individual's life. The ever-changing outer world gradually teaches a person to look for and appreciate inner, more lasting values. Ultimately each person is led to the realization that only his or her inner spirit remains untouched by change. The innermost nature of our Being remains steadfast through all passing joys and pains. It is at the core of our Being that our lives touch the Eternal, and it is from here that we derive our true strength.

OUR TRUE
STRENGTH

Deep within abides another life, not like
the life of the senses, escaping sight,
unchanging. This endures when all
created things have passed away.

Hinduism

The peace of God, which passeth all
understanding, shall keep your hearts and
minds.

Christianity

God is our refuge and strength, a very
present help in trouble. Therefore will not
we fear, though the earth be removed,
and though the mountains be carried into
the midst of the sea.

Judaism

Be lamps unto yourselves. Be a refuge
unto yourselves. Seek not for refuge from
anything but the Self. Desires and
tendencies pass away. Only the Self
abides.

Buddhism

Make honesty thy steed, truth thy saddle,
continence thine equestrian armor, the
five virtues thine arrows, and truth thy
sword and shield.

Sikhism

GOD IS
LOVE

In effect, this is the summation of all previous principles: God, the all-pervading oneness of spirit, is seen in essence as love.

The saints and sages of all religions have declared that they have drawn their wisdom from a universal source, and that this source is full of unbounded love and joy.

When believed and understood, the conviction that God is love will unite people everywhere.

GOD IS
LOVE

God is love, and he who abides in love
abides in God, and God abides in him.

Christianity

He that loveth not, knoweth not God.
For God is love.

Buddhism

Love is the beginning and end of the
Torah.

Judaism

Love belongs to the high nobility of
Heaven, and is the quiet home where
man should dwell.

Confucianism

Sane and insane, all are searching lovelorn
For Him, in mosque, temple, church,
    alike.
For only God is the One God of Love,
And Love calls from all these, each one
    His home.

Sufism

MAN IS CREATED
IN GOD'S IMAGE

God is love, and man is made in God's image. How easy it is to be caught in the difficulties of life and forget the basic underlying truths that are simple and straightforward.

Even in the midst of our busy world there are saints and sages working ceaselessly to infuse these simple truths into our complex lives. These noble souls radiate the divinity that is the inner basis of man's existence.

Regular periods of meditation and prayer will center us in the awareness of the underlying truths, so that we can recognize the divine within ourselves and radiate this understanding to others around us.

MAN IS CREATED
IN GOD'S IMAGE

God created man in His own image, in
the image of God created He him.

Judaism

The individual soul is nothing else in
essence than universal soul.

Hinduism

On God's own nature has been molded
man's.

Islam

God is concealed in every heart; his light
is in every heart.

Sikhism

Know ye not that ye are the temple of
God, and that the Spirit of God dwelleth
in you?

Christianity

LIVING IN
UNITY

Fostering growth and development is as natural to a society as desiring advancement in life is to an individual. The greater the harmony and peace in a nation, the greater is the opportunity for firmly established financial, spiritual, and educational organizations to develop. These organizations allow individuals and the society as a whole to progress.

The joy of living in society is that each person can derive benefits from every other person's efforts. Each person contributes a little, and then receives the vast benefit of society's achievements.

Material needs and comforts are only one aspect of this collective benefit; a greater aspect is the collective wisdom of the spiritual truths that are passed from generation to generation. This wisdom serves as a practical basis for achieving fulfillment in life.

LIVING IN UNITY

God hath made of one blood all nations
of men.

Christianity

Behold, how good and pleasant it is when
brothers dwell in unity!

Judaism

All creatures are the family of God; and
he is the most beloved of God who does
most good unto His family.

Islam

Human beings all are as head, arms,
trunk, and legs unto one another.

Hinduism

Do not forget that the world is one great
family.

Shintoism

PRAYERS OF THE RELIGIONS

The prayers of the world's religions have a common theme: the desire and need to make contact with God, and to be shown by Him the path on earth that leads to freedom, health, prosperity, and knowledge.

At its core, religion is extremely practical; its purpose is to lead mankind to greater happiness, achievement, and inner peace. These are the things that every person wants. These aspirations are the goals of life.

The central prayers of the religions ask for guidance in achieving these aspirations. Their common goal shows the essential oneness of the human spirit.

PRAYERS OF THE
RELIGIONS

Our Father who art in heaven, Hallowed be thy name. Thy kingdom come, Thy will be done, On earth as it is in heaven. Give us this day our daily bread; And forgive us our debts, As we also have forgiven our debtors; And lead us not into temptation, But deliver us from evil. Amen.

Christianity

Lead me, O Lord, in Thy righteousness. Make Thy way straight before me. Cleanse Thou me from hidden faults. Keep back Thy servant from presumptuous sins; let my sins not have dominion over me . . . Show me Thy ways, O Lord. Teach me Thy paths, and lead me in Thy truth. Thou art the God of my salvation.

Judaism

Praise be to God, the Lord of all
creatures; the most merciful, the king of
the day of judgment. Thee do we
worship, and of thee do we beg
assistance. Direct us in the right way, in
the way of those to whom thou hast been
gracious; not of those against whom thou
art incensed, nor of those who go astray.

Islam

Supreme Lord! Lord of warmth and light,
Of life and consciousness, that knows all,
Guide us by the right path to happiness,
And give us strength and will to war
     against
The sins that rage in us and lead us
     astray.
We bow in reverence and prayer to Thee.
     Aum.

Hinduism

Aum! Amīn! Āmēn! Amen!

CHRONOLOGY

The Vedic Texts of India
(Hinduism). . . . . *c.* 4500–3000 B.C.

Krishna, Hindu Deity . . . . . *c.* 1500 B.C.

Shinto Texts (Oral tradition
dates back to prehistoric
Japan). . . . . *c.* 1500–1000 B.C.

Judaism . . . . *c.* 1300 B.C.

Moses. . . . . *c.* 1300 B.C.

King Solomon . . . . *c.* 970 B.C.

The Upanishads of
Hinduism. . . . . *c.* 700–500 B.C.

Lao Tse, Principle Founder
of Taoism . . . . 604–515 B.C.

Mahavira, Principle Founder
of Jainism . . . . Born *c.* 600 B.C.

Buddha . . . . 573–483 B.C.

Confucious . . . . 551–479 B.C.

Socrates . . . . *c.* 470–399 B.C.

Plato. . . . . 429–348 B.C.

Mencius, Chinese contributor
to Confucianism . . . . *c.* 370–290 B.C.

Jesus. . . . . 5 B.C.–A.D. 30

123

SOURCES

Ballou, Robert O., ed. *The Bible of the World.* New York: The Viking Press, 1939.

Champion, Selwyn Gurney, and Short, Dorothy. *Readings from World Religions.* Boston: The Beacon Press, 1951.

Das, Bhagavan. *The Essential Unity of All Religions.* Wheaton, Ill.: The Theosophical Press, 1939.

Frost, S.E. Jr., ed. *The Sacred Writings of the World's Greatest Religions.* New York: McGraw-Hill, 1943.

Gaer, Joseph. *The Wisdom of the Living Religions.* New York: Dodd, Mead & Company, 1956.

The Holy Bible. King James Version.

The Holy Bible. Revised Standard Version.

The Koran. Trans. George Sale. Philadelphia: J.B. Lippincott & Co., 1864.

Legge, James, D.D., L.L.D. *The Life and Works of Mencius.* London: Trübner and Co., 1875.

Macauliffe, Max Arthur. *The Sikh Religion: Its Gurus, Sacred Writings and Authors.* Vol. 1. Bombay, India: Oxford University Press, 1963.

Oriental Literature: The Literature of China (Including the Analects of Confucius). Rev. ed. New York: The Colonial Press, 1900.

The Sacred Books of China: The Texts of Taoism. Trans. James Legge. London: Oxford University Press, 1891.

Sacred Books of the East (Including the Vedic Hymns and The Dhammapada of Buddhism). Rev. ed. New York: P.F. Collier & Sons, 1900.

ABOUT THE AUTHOR

JEFFREY MOSES has an M.A. in the philosophy of education from the University of Colorado. A freelance writer and advertising executive, Moses has spent the last ten years researching the world's great scriptures. He has traveled across the country lecturing to college and business people on the benefits of meditation and stress reduction techniques.

Jeffrey Moses lives with his wife, Ruth, in Fairfield, Iowa.